Reflections

by
Cathy Maertens

ISBN: 0-9719687-0-5

Library of Congress Control Number: 2002091951

The front cover photo was taken by the author of Lake Superior in
Duluth, Minnesota.
The back cover photo of the author was taken at Unique Portrait
Design Studio in St. Cloud, Minnesota.

Additional copies of this book are available by mail. Send $11.25
each (includes tax and postage) to:
Cathy Maertens
P.O. Box 355
Waite Park, Minnesota 56387-0355

Comments about the book may be sent to the same address and will
receive a response.

Printed in the United States by:
Morris Publishing
3212 East Highway 30
Kearney, NE 68847
1-800-650-7888

This book is dedicated
to our Lord who wrote
these poems through
my hand and my heart.

Acknowledgements

Special thanks to my very good friend, Mike Lundberg, who believed enough in me to help finance the first printing of this book.

Special thanks to my friends, Kristina Achmann and Christine Schaffers, who helped type some poems in preparation for publishing.

Special thanks to Unique Portrait Design for the use of a photograph of the author.

Contents

Rainbow

Oh, 'bow, why do you hide
where my heart cannot hear
the laughter in your lovely voice
as you speak and softly silence the rain?

I am lying on a layer of life
lonely and low in this high, empty place;
crying and craving with all my soul
to behold the beauty of your face.

Still you stay so far away
always and ever beyond my touch.
Never knowing I am here
or that I care so very much.

The desperate clouds cling one to another
without your light to keep them warm;
'til all at once together we cry
and somehow still survive the storm.

Watching, waiting with hopeful heart
I forever search the heavens above;
looking longingly on and on
reaching for my rainbow of love.

Sweet Dreams

I wish for you sweet dreams
For it is only the dreamer
who dares survive.

All the storms and struggles
will surely win
if the dream suddenly dies.

It takes every effort
all courage – all strength
and the fight goes on.

When we are in darkness
and the black walls surround us –
we need to go on.

Go on believing and always retrieving
those hopes and
all of our dreams.

It is only the dreamer
who looks for the love
and understands what living really means.

Flight

Golden hues of sun's rays past;
embers stretch across the sky.
You draw near on lighted wings;
descend; and rest upon mind's eye.

Gentle beauty - ever nearer
sweetest spirit shining bright.
Hold me tenderly and whisper
loving words throughout this night.

Sparkling - your eyes so tender,
passion's softest, finest light.
Memories - the wings of life -
take me now upon your flight.

Searching, soaring high upon
stars and galaxies divine.
The peace of even stillness lay
between your heart and soul and mine.

Tears and trembling;
to the place at last -
alone where two hearts dwell.
Brilliant joy with you beside me -
mortal words could never tell.

Worldly melodies surrender
to the angel voices dear;
choirs swell - the radiant splendor
of your spirit oh, so near.

The stars are fading -
soul descends
as rest gives way
to morning light.
I linger for a moment longer
with the beauty of the night.

Wings of flight descend -
surrender.
The rising sun doth steal my light.
Goodbye, my love,
until forever
when eternal is my night.

Christmas Poem

They say that Christmas time is magic
that there's something in the air.
It's the time when people come together
and show how much they care.

I've walked along the bustling streets
and looked for that holiday cheer.
I've searched their faces
yet have seen no traces
that Christmas will soon be here.

Their faces are troubled, tired, and tense.
They seem to be filled with despair.
To find the gift they can afford
they search everywhere.

I guess we've placed too much importance
on the material part of the season.
We give and we get and we celebrate,
but we have forgotten the reason.

Maybe it's time we took the time
to take a little time out,
to remember what it means to us.
What is Christmas all about?

We say it's the day our Lord was born.
We've known that from the start.
We know it in our head,
but do we feel it in our heart?

I know that when I feel it most,
when I feel that Jesus is near,
is when I'm with the ones I love,
with the people I hold dear.

I see Him very clearly
in their smiles and in their sighs.
I see Him when I look at you
in the love that's in your eyes.

No, it's not the trees, the presents,
the cards, the fireplace, or the snow.
It's the love that sets the day apart.
It's the fire from an inner glow.

Oh yes, Christmas time is special –
we smile, we laugh, we love, we play,
but with you I feel the magic of Christmas
every single day.

The Clock

All of her friends with their foolish fun,
their lives just begun,
she's the only one
who's old at heart.

She listens to the lovely laughter,
the pitter-patter of the rain,
memories cause her pain,
and the clock is ticking.

Before, the rain did fall,
but after all, she had her bow
and wouldn't ya know
she cherished that love in her heart.

Now she listens to the skies weep,
her sighs are deep,
she longs to sleep,
and the clock is ticking.

Long lives the light,
but to her it is night,
and she buries the lost love
which is her right,
and heavy is her heart.

She listens to the rumbling thunder,
while tears are falling,
someone is calling,
and the clock is ticking.

The birds still sing and everything,
but the world to her
is but a blur,
creates no stir,
and there is no cure
for a broken heart.

She listens to the lightning splitting,
and as it pours,
the thunder roars,
her soul soars,
and the clock stopped.

Sister Poem

As I look out over the lake
and watch the setting sun,
I recall the day's events -
all the things that I have done.

I've worked; I've played;
I've given my best;
I've filled and enjoyed the hours.
I patted the cat and took the time
to see and to smell the flowers.

My life is full and satisfying
and I know I should be happy,
but there's a tear upon my face –
there is something that's lacking.

I feel an emptiness inside
which I, alone, can't fill.
It has always lingered there
and I guess it always will.

The feeling that no matter the number
of people surrounding me –
in my heart is a place for one
who was never meant to be.

I wanted her in my life.
I wanted her to be born.
And so although she never lived,
it is for her I mourn.

I needed her so many times
to listen and understand.
I needed her to comfort me –
reach out and take my hand.

I needed her to laugh with
and talk to about personal things.
About the flowers and the kittens
and the thrill a first date brings.

I had so much to share with her -
my thoughts, my sports, my songs.
With her I'd feel I was complete -
accepted - like I belong.

But when I prayed; the Lord said "No,
there will be but one in your home."
And so I feel the emptiness
of living life alone.

And it is for her I grieve
and why I am so sad.
I need and love and miss so much
the sister I never had.

Touching

Blow, gentle breezes, blow
to the corners of my soul.
Take away the dirt within
'til I'm pure and clean again.

By the lovely lake I sigh
as the waves go rolling by,
and I think of younger days
when I had much milder ways.

When this simple beauty before me
was enough to send me soaring
high and free and feeling close
to my God - the Lord of hosts.

How the tears do moisten now
and the sweat pours on my brow -
as I fight to keep control -
not wanting to see what I already know.

Look how far this girl has come.
She no longer shines with the sun.
She's the cloud ready to burst
with the world and all of its thirst.

Who can quench the thirst so strong?
Will this world? Does she belong?
How to turn back - yet go on
and capture the peace, the joy, the song?

Where is the song - still in her heart?
Yes, still there, yet torn apart.
The pieces lay and patiently wait
for some redemption or hand of fate.

This is her moment - the time has come.
The tears - the heart - He has won.
Yes, Lord, I know I belong to you -
the only real peace - the love that's true.

Suddenly, pieces begin to fit
-tie together - a perfect knit.
No longer broken and torn apart.
He has come to heal my heart.

Blow, you gentle breezes, blow;
touch the places of my soul.
Holy Spirit help me know
of His love which makes me whole.

I feel His power and saving grace,
and I can almost see His face.
Smiling, tender, loving me.
I am soaring, I am free.

The sun is shining with me now,
the cloud is gone and I know how
to quench the thirst - the need for love.
I have only to look above.

Blow, you gentle breezes, blow
to the millions of souls
thirsting for your cleansing power
in their lost and lonely hour.

Reflections

The evening sky
the changing hues-
from lighter shades
to darker blues.

The hours moving-
the changing clocks,
waiving the moments-
tic tock-tic tock.

Time and nature
moving forward.
Ever changing
ever slowly.

And what of myself?
Am I evolving?
As I sit
with the world revolving?

Or am I still
that troubled spirit-
who spoiled the day
and everyone in it?

By smearing mistrust
and the green-eyed creature
on the table of flowers
and cakes left to greet her?

The darkness falls
on both sides now
I see it within-
and I see it without.

The choice to forgive-
not to judge nor dismay.
I regret not making
that choice this day.

The sun has gone now
down deep in the west.
The anger has changed
to depression at rest.

Love-as the darkness
outside and around me
brings me some pain
yet hope does surround me.

For while our time
and our nature does change;
hurt and regrets
cannot love rearrange.

The love is a constant
and cannot depart,
though pain shares it's space
this night in two hearts.

There will be forgiveness.
There will be more pain.
More light and more darkness;
and the seasons will change.

Evenings into twilight-
summers into fall.
Yet love is love
is love over all.

The Unquenchable Thirst of a Broken Heart

Weight drags, for half is dead
while bit by bit
the brave boulder crumbles.

Precious pictures of the past play
while pain stabs, steals
and severs.

Frustration, feelings, and fury fly
while cries carve holes
of helplessness and hunger.

Moments move
while days dwindle -
a death - a silence.

Surrender solemnly quiets shared
laughter, love, and life
while sadness spreads
the cover of cold.

Smiles spark the soul
while tender touch
turns matches to flames.

Flames mingle
while fire melts
a frozen pond to pools of sorrow.

Thousands upon thousands
of silent drops fall
forming an ocean
while rivers flow freely again,
yet never fulfill nor satisfy
"The Unquenchable Thirst".

A Sister's Love

With every sun that rises east -
soft and warm and bright,
your love is shining with the dawn
of memory's sweet light.

The winds do blow among the woods
and gently they caress.
Your soothing touch embraces me
and calms my fears to rest.

As Mother Nature, always present,
'though sometimes silent she,
so you are with me all my days,
'though sometimes silently.

The ocean waves flow in and out
upon the sandy shore.
So, too, our journey ebbs and tides,
apart, then close once more.

And with each setting sun that glows
and brings the close of day,
a sister's love is burning bright
forever and always.

Questions

As I come all alone
to the church to pray,
I think of the people
I've met on life's way.

The Rainbow, Wild Woman,
and the angels in disguise,
the half-truths, the pretense,
the masks, and the lies.

It was all a dream,
too good to be real,
and now once again
I'm afraid to feel.

I wonder why they used me
and then let me go?
If only I had not
loved them all so.

And I wonder why You let them
toss me aside? To make me humble?
Did I have too much pride?
Because I thought of them
more often than You?
Or do You want me to go on
and find someone new?

Will there ever be someone
who really cares?
Someone with whom I can share
all of myself - all my life -
all my love? Or must I wait,
Lord, 'til I'm with You up above?

I know I should love You
above all the others -
more than my friend, family, or lover.
But, Lord, I get lonely once in a while
without a soft touch or a friendly smile.

I need someone with me day after day
to hold me, to love me, to show me the way.
I know I will find him, Lord, in your time.
Then I will be his and he will be mine.

And we will be one with You as our guide.
We'll open our home and let You come inside.
Until then I'll try to be gentle and kind.
With peace in my heart I will have peace of mind.

And whenever I feel troubled, tired, or bored,
I'll talk with You, my very best friend,
my dear Lord.
You listen, You care, and You understand.
You smile and You take me by the hand.

And I feel You now as I sit and pray.
Your wisdom and love have shown me the way.
My heart that was heavy – now is so light.
I thank You for helping me in my plight.

I thank You, I praise You,
I respect You too.
But most of all, Lord,
I really love You.

Burial

Oh, you candle, softly burning
with the tears upon your sides-
Please burn quickly- oh, so quickly,
and end these years of mournful sighs.

You whom I sent with love and hope
thinking that two flames were burning.
Yet the warmth did meet with cold
and left me weeping and yearning.

Yearning for that other flame
which my own will someday greet.
We'll mingle and then flare with force
and quench what water cannot meet.

Burn, I say, burn quickly now.
Wipe the former far away.
Let your ashes become the stone
and let me rise to a new day.

Burn thyself down to the ground
and be gone, then, from my sight.
Take with thee former illusions,
while they live they are my plight.

But remember to burn brightly
and proclaim with fiery blasts
the love I still feel for them.
For the love will forever last.

And let your sweet scent linger
after the fire has been spent.
As my soul searches onward
past the hearts of discontent.

I sadly watch you die before me,
candle of misguided trust.
Yet body banished- your spirit remains
just as all true love must.

Now as your final flicker fades
into the darkness of this night,
I see the hope shining before me-
the hope of tomorrow's lasting light.

Goodbye

As she trudges up the stairs
feeling the weight of one,
she tries to hide, but knows inside
that the waiting has just begun.

The heart that pounds so strongly
and deeply within her chest
will surely rob her of peace
and interfere with rest.

Such a heart is hard to bear
and she often wonders why
our Lord has given this to her?
And she remembers the goodbye.

How the joy did swell and flow
throughout her every vein,
when after waiting patiently,
she saw her friend again.

What love and joy were hers this day!
Such laughter, love, and peace!
To speak, to listen, to be understood
by her dear friend, Therese.

How cruel it is to have to bear
the pain that follows love.
It seems to fall so quickly
as the rain pours from above.

As the ashes follow fire,
yet a spark or two remains,
a hope does keep her love alive -
the hope of togetherness again.

But as for now, she slowly climbs
the stairway to her room.
That very place not long ago
had really felt like home.

Just a taste - a bit of heaven
that is all one heart can take.
Only so much joy or sorrow
and then it surely will break.

Is that why He gives her only
a little time to say hello?
Would it be too great a blessing
if she never did have to let go?

Perhaps the sorrow is the easier
of the two for her to bear?
"Practice often makes for perfect".
Could she live without a care?

Oh, the joys her heart can hold
and the wonderful peace of mind
of loving another so deeply,
a love of the truest kind.

But, oh, dear Father, help her now
to bear the tears and the sighs,
and the broken loneliness
of this sad goodbye.

My Year in Moorhead

It was a trip that had no end.
I was alone and needed a friend.
But friends fade in the light of day.
Dreams die and are swept away.

I faced a sea of empty faces,
and entered strange and evil places.
The wave rolled closer
and brought me sorrow,
the wave of reality,
the worries of tomorrow.

The wind was wild, but even still
my love stayed warm despite the chill.
And after tears had been shed,
these thoughts were still in my head.

How to help them look above
to find the peace, the joy, the love.
To mourn losses; to cry out in pain;
to weep or wail; to walk in the rain.

To remember days that long had past;
to cling to things you thought would last;
to feel the weight of being alive;
to struggle and sweat just to survive.

To hear the silent cry of those
who do pretend, but inside know
that the fierce and fearless life they lead
hides a heart that burns and bleeds -

For something, someone to love and care,
someone with whom they could share
what's deep inside - the hunger, the need,
so at last they could be freed.

Freed from their pride - the powerful drape
that draws to close, to cover their ache.
How deep is their hurt?
Their need to love?
God only knows.
For they walk in sleep behind the drape,
and darkness fills their souls.

In Memory of Lauri

I say to the soft, sensitive souls:
"Never listen to the ones
who kill a love so beautiful
with their green hearts and evil tongues".

I now tell you of my tale,
while speaking to a dear old friend.
The tale of heavenly happiness
with a heartache from hell at the end.

Come to me and let me hear you,
when we waken in the dark
with our surface penetrated,
in the coals there is a spark.

Come to me and let me know you
while the warm rays filter through
our eyes, our souls, our everything.
The light reveals what is true.

Come to me and let me show you
all the love I have inside.
In the secret room we wander
'though we have nothing to hide.

Come to me and let me hold you
while the burning blazes past
the words, the whispers, now the walls
are falling, falling, falling fast.

Come to me and let me love you
with the time we have to touch.
The flame flickers, the world snickers,
oh, our love is just too much.

Too much, too strong, too deep, too pure.
The world has brought us to an end.
They killed what was so beautiful.
They have buried my forever friend.

Searching

Cries in the darkness
tears in our eyes
no one will see us
no one will try.

Caught in a blur
of selfish tasks
they are too busy
and no one will ask.

Faces the same
no special ones there
no one to touch you
no one to care.

Outsiders watching
the others at play,
yes, we are fooled
and continue to pray.

Praying for answers
for one heart that's true,
funny, I could've sworn
it was you.

But wishes and dreams
and prayers without end
will do us no good
if we all end up dead.

What is the limit?
Is there a light?
Something to hope for
to get through the night?

Rebellion arises,
but no release there.
It's bottled and burning
won't someone care?

Hearts seem so happy
on faces I see -
my beats - they differ
and there's no one for me.

Prayer may prolong
me now until dawn,
but soon it'll come -
when I can no longer hold on.

Betrayal

"Whatever is the matter?"
Oh, no, surely you jest?
To lose a man - as if that
would take away my best.

No, it is with sadder heart
I claim the very reason.
A blow not of enemy - but of friend
has injured me with treason.

What courage I had upon to call
to ask for help and cry.
To put myself at mercy
yet away with face and pride.

Then - your response (the hypocritical yes)
to give me falsest hope.
To then use anger as your sword
to slowly cut my throat.

You cut my throat - no more to cry
or trust or murmur endearments.
For your betrayal of my heart
leaves me now in torment.

So stand you there - unbelievable innocence
asking yet how I am.
You who think paleness of heart
is caused only by man.

A man is mere flesh -
while the spirit is all -
and spirit's no gender by preference.
For love takes to heart
and what'ere form can hold
to sustain or to slay you -
no difference.

Life at the Hoodechecks

The day is like a river
rapidly flowing.
The words and the shouting -
people coming and going.

The house like a log
crashing up against the rocks,
bears the burden of slams,
phone calls, and door knocks.

The cat is our island,
he's always around;
while we are sailing
he has his feet on the ground.

Evening is the tide
that is ebbing away.
We slow down and unwind
at the end of the day.

The night is the land
where we harbor our boat.
But at times we break loose
and begin to float.

The waters become wild
and we lose control.
We ride waves of desire
until we make our way home.

But the moments I cherish,
the nights I feel blessed,
are the ones when we place
ourselves at rest.

When our anchor is strong
and the water is still.
When we are together
and take time to feel.

In those quiet nights
it is somehow enough
to be still and share
our soft, silent love.

Running

Water. Running away.
Mind on the move.
Muscles move on mud.
Water on my face -
is it from within?
From without?
Without what?
Lost it - the love.

Black smears my hands.
I see the running streaks.
I put them on my cheeks.
Oh, how my face leaks.
Why cry "why"?
Lost it - the time.

Brown - my white socks.
Red - my sore eyes.
I see the stain.
I hear the cries.
I smell the rain
running from the skies.
Too late to run - no reason why.
Lost it - the Rainbow.

Water. Still running.
Soul is up.
My throat opens -
what is there?
Words saying what?
No more - no way.
Nothing but pain.
Lost it - the love.

Water running from His side.
Red - the sign of His love.
Bright is the hope.
Strong is the faith
that keeps the thrill;
that calms the cries;
that destroys the fears;
that cleanses the soul;
that consoles the sorrowing;
that treasures the love.
Always will have it -
His love.

The Laughter of Pain

She always has a crazy joke
and a grin upon her face.
And of sadness, sorrow, or tears
there never is a trace.

She moves too fast;
she hides too well;
she laughs too much;
for them to tell.

But beneath her happy
and joking side
lies loneliness –
someone who cries.

Someone who wants
so much to be loved –
she's afraid to reveal
all the things she's made of.

What she does not see,
but really should know
is that even without
all of the show –

We love her so much
or, at least, I do.
So, now when she laughs,
I may not laugh too.

Because I have seen
looking into her eyes
that the laughter and jokes
are sometimes a lie.

And when sorrow calls
she washes out the rain -
Not with her tears,
but with a laughter of pain.

Rainbow Lost

Oh, 'bow, why do you abide
where my heart cannot find it?
The treasure of your beauty you hide
which surpasses all possessions.

I am lying to the clouds
built of black sins and stained.
Burned and blank, through mist
I strained to see your light
after it rained.

But the darkness alone remains
as somehow I knew it would.
To catch a glimpse and feel your warmth.
Oh, if only somehow I could.

The air is troubled inside these clouds,
they tremble; chilled, they break;
and cold drops of lonely tears
fall down upon my ache.

I could search amid my pain
for your love in heavens above,
and yet I know 'twould be in vain.
I've looked and looked -
there's only the rain.

Friendship

I don't desire gifts or flowers.
I just want to spend my hours
being close to you.

I don't need words of wisdom
or intellectual stimulation.
I just need those warm vibrations
from your shining smile and caring eyes.

I don't wish for us to spend
all of our time running blindly
from one event to another.
I just want to discover
all I possibly can about you.

So just give me love and hold me close
as that is what I love the most
about being your friend.

And I'll try and do the same
and bring you more pleasure than pain,
but through both sunshine and rain
know that: " I Love You."

Soul Pull

There is a drawing that occurs
between the souls of men
which is rare and wonderful
and somehow transcends -

the mere surface attraction
of the body and the flesh.
It occurs when two hearts
entwine and mesh -

so perfectly; it is so right
and in no way wrong.
You wonder how without the other
you ever got along?

It's like you came alive -
began breathing that very moment when
you first saw your love.
You try, but cannot pretend -

that it did not stir your soul
with every touch and glance.
To try and forget this love -
there never was a chance.

It is nothing like the lust
of this mortal world.
They would never comprehend it
and there just are no words -

To tell them what you feel
when your soul sees mine.
It's like we exist all alone
in our own space and time.

It is not your lips nor your face
which has drawn me nigh.
It is but the look that I see
when I gaze into your eyes.

You tell me I am not wrong
to want and love you so;
and yet I see you telling me
that you do want me to go.

The world is killing
the one beautiful force
that is left upon this earth.
They are pulling and tearing at our love
because there is no birth.

So we now dwell in separate shells
never to be one.
Yet that drawing of our souls
cannot be undone.

It remains forever in us
searching endlessly -
to find a way, dear God, some way
that it can be free.

Our flesh is silent - wanting nothing;
yet our spirits cry to touch,
and be united once again
with the one we love so much.

Perhaps, dear one, if God allows
we'll meet in heaven above,
and there the drawing forces within us
can live forever in love.

Christmas

Tinsel, trees, and mistletoe,
toys and candy and ho! ho! ho!
Santa gently rocks a child,
Christmas carols all the while.

Lights shining upon the snow,
Christmas stockings in a row.
All the signs of holiday cheer.
I know that Christmas must be near.

Garland and stars above the fire,
cards received and sent.
A pretty wreath to admire
and fill the house with holiday scents.

December 24 the calendar shows.
We've even gotten our Christmas snow.
Church bells ring and carolers sing,
yet I am missing something.

The presents are empty
without the smiles
and the joy of visiting
for a while.

And it's just not
Christmas time for me
until my sweet mother and father
I see.

Yes, bring on your trees
and your mistletoe,
but the love is the Christmas
I've come to know.

Christmas is love and family
and that's all that really
matters to me.

No matter the date
nor the hour of time,
no greater gift
is more sublime.

And it really isn't
Christmas for me
until my dear parents
are here with me.

An Angel's Voice

Amid the clamor of life
an angel's voice I hear.
It is the voice of my
sweet mother - Zoe Degraer.

With her quaint Belgian accent,
she murmurs gentle words.
I learn of her joys in life:
card games, flowers, and birds.

Never a harsh word is spoken
to judge nor condemn.
Whomever speaks with Zoe
has found an honest friend.

Her comforting words of wisdom
have guided me as a youth;
and now they bless my children
with grace, love, and truths.

The following five poems
are dedicated to the many
victims of domestic abuse
in this country and to
their loved ones who often
suffer right along with them.
A fictitious victim's name
has been used for the
purpose of this book.

Dear Linda,

What have I done
to be so blessed
with my friend, Linda,
whom I love the best?

Warmth, kindness,
and laughter abound.
The bond is deep
and love surrounds me.

She calls me her angel
yet she is the one
the Lord smiles upon
when day is done.

Accepting my faults
she brings out my best.
No wonder I love her
above all the rest.

Nothing I have done
nor will ever do
will bring me such joy
as loving you,

dear Linda.

She Called Me Her Angel

Remember when I was your angel,
your sister, and your friend?
We laughed, we cried, and we talked
about everything back then.

I remember being your angel, girl.
Yet it seems so long ago.
I was happy when you married -
how was I to know?

You whispered sweetly in my ear
and you held me tight.
How I wish I could go back
and relive those nights.

How can he be so cruel to you
when you are so kind?
My heart is aching, I long to be
your angel one more time.

I'd lift you up to where you'd
never suffer from his touch.
Then you'd be safe and free to laugh
with the ones you love so much.

Through prayer I must be lifting you
to heights you've never known.
And with God's mercy and His grace
your angel will bring you home.

Deliverance

I cannot reach her,
I cannot find
the way to alter
her troubled mind.

I cannot break
his strong control
which breaks my heart
and imprisons her soul.

How much more sorrow?
How much more pain?
Until she's safe
and free again?

God, I love her.
God, help her.
Be her answer.
Be her cure.

Be with her, Lord,
I must trust you
to do the things
I cannot do.

Be her angel.
Be her friend.
For my time with her
has reached its end.

Watch her closely,
hold her tight.
Help her make it
through this night.

Sing to her
a lullaby.
Ease her pain
whenever she cries.

Wipe her tears
gently away.
Give her hope.
Help her to pray.

Give her courage.
Give her sight.
Please, God, help her
see the light.

Warm her heart
and protect her soul.
Keep her hoping.
Keep her whole.

Hold her, love her,
keep her warm.
Dear God,
keep her safe from harm.

My Prayer

I've never seen a mountain
nor tasted salty ocean air,
but I've had a lot of joy in life,
and many friends with which to share.

I don't need a lot of money -
never had much from the start,
but I wish I could be richer
where it matters - in my heart.

So, if I had just one wish
to be granted before I go -
I would like to spend more time
with one friend whom I loved so.

Because each day I spend without her
is a little sadder than the one before;
though many people do surround me -
there is a longing for one more.

One more time to see her smile
and let me know 'everything's okay'.
One more time with her arms around me -
it is for these things I pray.

If I never see a mountain
nor taste the ocean's salty air
I really will not mind a bit.
I can honestly say, " I just don't care".

Because love has already taken me
to the highest mountaintop
where the wonder and the beauty
never seemed to stop.

I don't need to taste the ocean air
nor gaze across an endless sea.
I've already felt the endless love
that she once had for me.

So, if there is a God in heaven,
and I truly believe there is -
then one day before I die
I know that He will grant me this:

To see her smile; hear her laughter;
and feel her gentle touch.
To feel - just one more time
the love I miss so much.

The Struggle

I see her face.
I can't erase
these feelings in my heart.

They seem to stay -
try as I may;
they will not depart.

Her loyal words of friendship linger
like an after-taste.
The bitter-sweet -
I must retreat -
the nightmare is reality.

Every joy is lessened now.
Every sorrow doubled.
I cannot laugh
without the guilt
of knowing she's in trouble.

Only in prayer
there is some peace
and I can retrieve
my sense of self
and alas
some of what I _need_.

In prayer is hope -
a chance to breathe.
I know my needs
have been decreed
and truly I must
leave her to heaven.

Jessica

Who is this girl
who is so kind?
Who gently holds
her hands in mine?
I can only guess.

Who is this girl
with the soulful eyes
who has taken me quite by surprise?
I see her name is Jess.

She's telling me
about her strife
as if I've known her
all my life.
I'm learning about this Jess.

Afraid of getting hurt,
I try and hide,
but she manages
to get inside
my heart.
And I want to protect this Jess.

She makes me laugh
and makes me see
how special she is.
Now she's special to me.
I think I love you, Jess.

Already I know
I want her to be
more than a friend
more like family.
Will you be my sister, Jess?

When you touched my hands
I didn't know your name.
Now you've touched my heart
and I'll never be the same.
I'll love you forever,
my sweet sister, Jess.

Golden Moments

We share golden moments
treasures untold.
Each other to cherish
as our lives unfold.

Exploring new waters
laughter freely flows.
Expressing our thoughts -
connecting our souls.

Hearts overflowing -
it's almost too much.
Quite overwhelming
when our spirits touch.

So much in common -
so much more than friends.
A rare, special love -
one without end.

Gentle words whispered -
embraces so sweet.
Our sister bond strong,
yet we must retreat

to our separate worlds
and our separate lives.
Not quite yet -
not quite time.

Twilight approaches
a prayer sent for you.
Sunrise to sunset
another day through.

Our time will come -
golden moments extend.
My sister - my family -
a lifetime to spend.

God's Greatest Gift

I love the sunlight
on winters' snow,
and a candlelight's
soft, warm glow.

Twinkling stars
upon a velvet night,
and the promise of
first mornings' light.

Listening to the
bird's sweet song,
and the crickets chirping
all night long.

Rose petals
soft to the touch -
these things I do love
very much.

But I thank God for you
when on my knees,
for I love you
so much more than these.

And nothing in this world
comes close
to my little sister
whom I love the most.

Dreaming

When the hard days have no end,
and the night is just too long,
I think of you, my sweet sister, Jess,
and dream sweet dreams until dawn.

When the world was cruel to you,
and your tears began to fall,
how I held you; how I loved you;
my heart was breaking with it all.

Now when the world does bring me down,
and I need you desperately,
sweet memories of yesterdays
bring you close to me.

So, when the nights are long and dark,
I know I can hold on.
Your smile - your touch -
your tender love
brings the brightest dawn.

The Way

"Not for my glory, Lord,
but so Thy will be done"
In that single moment how
He all the world had won.

Not with power of His hand,
but in the heart of one divine.
Having all yet having none -
giving Himself as bread and wine.

How do we in contrast fail
to do as the Word was told?
And what are we to say to Him
when it's our time for growing old?

Drive, ambition, fierce control –
our will surpasses thoughts divine.
Our will, our way, our life:
not Yours, Lord, but mine.

There is but one above all else –
one hand, one heart, one mind
who is all loving and is worthy
of our love, our life, our time.

For Your glory, Lord, I pray
my life and soul are Yours.
Let Your thoughts, Your heart,
Your will be my sole reward.

Oh, dear Father, help me see
"The Way" that Jesus lived.
One way, one choice and then
all else will be forgiven.

At the twilight of the hour
as at the dawn of day,
still He calls us to His breast
to wipe our tears away.

Despite the torment we have caused Him
by our selfish, sinful deeds,
He remains and beckons now
and cares for all our needs.

Whose hand on this earth
can touch as gently as our Lord's?
Whose heart is pure and full and good
and deserves to adored?

No human heart nor hand compares
nor thought nor act of will.
All are but a grain of sand
or as a mountain to a hill.

I am in my noontime hour -
not at dusk or dawn.
I have time to do Your will
to which I feel most drawn.

If indeed I must choose
between this world and You,
then to Your will and Your way
oh Lord, I will be true.

For only then will happiness
and peace and glory live.
For we can only receive love
when we learn how to live it.

Choices

Smoothing back her hair -
one of her feminine moves.
Fingers reaching for the cross -
wondering which is true?

A part of her is woman
and perhaps a part's divine.
Will she ever know her calling?
And then will there be time?

Goals, dreams, realities.
This world and the next.
There really is no question
which one is the best.

Why, then, the worldly thoughts?
Why the womanly moves?
They seem at times irrelevant -
to threaten or intrude.

"To live for today and the present"
is the key.
We are now on earth
and the rest is mystery.

But belief remains
and the ever-present doubt.
Giving, getting, sharing -
what is it all about?

A woman, a man, a marriage.
A family, a child.
Worldly things and thoughts
can also be worthwhile.

Yet the vows of marriage
to our Lord somehow surpass
the other fine temptations,
and yet she has to ask;

Exactly what is right?
What is best for her?
Both of them will last -
the love of both endures.

Love - that is the answer
and either life will fit -
to set a good example
so others remember it.

Remember how Christ desires
for all of us to live.
Getting and celebrating (Yes),
and also knowing how to give.

And giving (in whatever form)
is the greatest expression of love.
The gift of money can be the same
as the smile or the hug.

Loving and the need to be loved.
We are human and divine.
Whatever style of living we choose
needs both the water and the wine.

She will know for certain one day
which path that she will take,
but as long as she lives in love
there'll be no mistake.

Faith

Looking - never seeing - yet the
sight is always there.
I search and I stumble
past unblinking, empty stares.

Outwardly appearing happy;
while inside I do strive
to find the face - to see the look
that will help me come alive.

I am battling with survivals' sea.
The view is blurred - the way is rough.
I stiffen and I stifle cries -
no time for tears - I must be tough.

Yet I cannot silence my cry
for there's a desperate need within
to feel the warmth - to fight for dreams
(No, I will not give in.)

Oh, the heart that has touched mine
while enduring the healing pain.
He suffered, forgave, and then died
so that we all might live again.

From my bleak and empty world
He took away the chill
with His hope, love, faith, and words.
Lord, I can hear You still.

He told us then and is calling now:
"Reach for the highest of heights.
Live in the love of the Lord
and you will be alright."

He still gives me the love I need
to strive for my desires.
He stirs the spark of dreams;
they wake; and then the flames
become a fire.

Touch a stranger and share.
Touch a friend and feel.
But touch a lover if you want to live;
then your dreams can become real.

He is a lover of hearts and life,
and touches all with His love.
It is His touch that brings me closer -
ever closer to our God of love.

It is true sometimes I fail Him,
but I believe that He still cares.
So, I look - never seeing;
yet the sight is always there.

Easter Poem

Winter's dreary gray shadows
cast across a barren land,
reflect the shadows of sin
which cloud the very soul of man.

Silent, sorrowful days to follow
Jesus' steps to Calvary
where He died for our sins
upon a cross to set us free.

Like the people of His day,
we, too, do scourge and spite Him.
We hurt our brothers and our sisters
with our pride and our fighting.

Winter's wind of frost and chill
over the silent earth does blow,
as our fighting chills the love
that in summer we did know.

Jesus, Son of the living God,
did not turn His face away.
He bore the cross, bled, and died,
and in dying He did say:

"Forgive them, Father, please forgive,
for they know not what they do".
So, we must say to one another:
"I will forgive you, too".

Winter's snow begins to melt.
It is the time to repent,
and ask God for forgiveness
through the forty days of Lent.

Finally, the gray departs
to reveal the glorious sun.
The entry of the cave is opened,
it's the resurrection of the Son.

The Son of God has arisen,
and out of the gray we see
brighter colors beckoning,
our hearts rejoice triumphantly.

Spring - the season of growth
with blooming buds under the sun.
Easter season of renewal -
growing together we become one.

We put behind our past offenses,
sins, and sorrows and rejoice
in God our Savior - let us praise Him
now together with one voice.

Our souls are cleansed,
there is springs' fresh dew.
Our spirits soar
with hopes renewed.

Now together we do sing,
celebrate, and praise as one
the crucified Christ who has arisen.
Glory to the living Son!

For joy, laughter, and peace.
For people everywhere we pray.
May all be blessed with love and hope
upon this holy Easter day.

Goodbye to the Hoodechecks

In the stillness of the night
I'm sitting here alone.
It's quiet now – dark in the house,
this house I call home.

It doesn't seem that long ago,
it seems like yesterday –
when I first came and then when I
decided I would stay.

The family was good to me.
Too good right from the start.
I didn't want to let them in,
but they entered into my heart.

The wind is softly whistling.
Could I but sing it's tune.
If only moments would not move,
then it never would be June.

I hear the purr of the cat.
Now he's crying for attention.
I wish I could be more like him
and put aside pretension.

I'm trying to distance myself from them
still I want to hold them close.
I am pushing them away
at a time I need them the most.

A moonbeam smiles in the darkness.
I am thankful for its light.
I see the smiles that sustained me
through the long and lonely nights.

Oh, it hasn't all been wine and roses.
We have had our share of pain.
There were times when we were angry,
but then we would make up again.

The seasons passed - first fall
then winter with all of it's fiery storms.
We fought the cold and together
somehow managed to stay warm.

It's springtime now and I know
so soon it will be summer.
Already I can sense the change
and I'm feeling the hunger.

Like the wind - always moving,
I, too, must move along.
There are obstacles to pass.
I know I must be strong.

Still, everywhere I look I see
a picture from the past.
I want to hold it and not let go.
I want to make it last.

I see Jenny, my dear friend,
with love soft in her eyes.
I'm trying to be so hard now
yet I'm the one who cries.

I cannot see anymore
after all these years.
I still cannot see the way
to look beyond the tears.

I cry these days deep inside -
very deep so she won't see.
I am not ready to let her know
how much she means to me.

I know that they all like me,
but she cares more than the rest.
And although I do love them all,
I do love her the best.

Sometimes I think it is because
I never had a sister,
but there are many more reasons why
I will really miss her.

Her very nature is so kind
and she was always there for me.
When I was lost and needed a friend
she held me tenderly.

No, I don't wish for fame or money.
I don't want to pay that price.
Nor do I wish for God to grant me
perfect joy or a really long life.

I simply look up to the Lord
and pray to the heavens above,
"Please don't let me live in a world
in which there is no love".

Now as I slip up to her room,
softly I hear her sigh.
I shut the door to shut her out.
Again I want to cry.

The other day she greeted me,
and I could sense her doubt.
I was strangely silent.
What was this all about?

Well, my friend, it is this way,
you see, my heart is breaking.
I do not know what to do
to ease the painful aching.

The hour is late and I am tired.
I really should be asleep.
If I can only close my eyes,
then perhaps they will not weep.

Even when my eyes give into
slumber so it seems,
they do not let me rest in peace.
I see you in my dreams.

It seems so very strange to me
how pain and love go together.
Someday this pain will leave me alone,
but the love will live on forever.

What Love Is

When I hear you laughing
and it makes me smile –
I know what joy is.

When I do something wrong
and you forgive me –
I know what compassion is.

When I do something
to make you happy
and you don't even know
it was me who did it –
I know what selflessness is.

When I show you
my faults and weaknesses
and you stand by me, anyway –
I know what acceptance is.

When you hurt me
and I take you back –
I know what forgiveness is.

When I miss you
even when a lot of people
are around me –
I know what loneliness is.

When I think of the years
we've spent together
and all the times
we've supported each other –
I know what friendship is.

When I look at you
and listen to my heart –
I know what love is.

Thank the Lord for You

I can see the strain and pain of those
who must struggle to get by.
As I watch the way you make them smile,
I almost start to cry.

When they are sad and have had
about as much as they can stand,
then you appear - you're always near
to lend a helping hand.

In the smoke they often joke
about the tragedies of life.
And yet you know that each blow
has cut them like a knife.

Some have tried hard to hide
their pain over the years,
but they have cried, and inside
you can see their river of tears.

When we frown and are down,
and our strength is almost gone,
when we need some hope just to cope
and help us carry on -

Then we look to you to see us through,
and our spirits start to rise.
You are always there and we know you care
by the love that's in your eyes.

And I swear when in prayer
I thank the Lord for you.
For every day and for every way
your love has seen us through.

Something Strong

I remember the days of toil and sweat.
They were really happy times.
And it's the smiles I see the most
when I go back there in my mind.

Oh, yeah, there was pain,
our common pain,
but it often helped to bind us.
And although it searched
and searched for us,
sorrow could not find us.

Something strong - so very strong,
wiped our tears away,
and filled us with peace and joy and life
and laughter for our days.

The something strong - so much stronger
than sorrow could ever be,
that turned our thoughts and souls
and hearts away from misery:

That special something in our midst
was a gift from God above.
What made us smile and made us laugh
was our deep and beautiful love.

We acted the way we all should act
toward our sisters and our brothers.
Being good not only to ourselves,
but being good to one another.

That is why it hurts to have to go
and leave you at this time,
but there's one thing that seems to help
so I try to keep it in mind.

I know that love is so much stronger
than any problem we may have to face,
and in life we take love along with us
as we travel from place to place.

Now I'm taking your love along with me
as I leave this - my second home.
And my love remains with all of you.
Noone is ever really alone.

The Show

Tension, laughter, jokes, and prayers.
Lines and movements and phrases.
A common goal, a bond, a touch.
A look of love upon your faces.

The interviews, pictures in the paper,
the lights, the set, the cast, the crew.
These set the stage, the curtain rises -
now all eyes are upon you.

A stirring inside - alert and ready.
"Practiced this a thousand times".
You come alive - blend heart with words
that are engraved within your mind.

Smooth and easy, softly flowing,
then building - breaking through the walls.
Conflict - drama - resolution.
You stand for the curtain call.

Holding hands and lifting hearts,
together you bow and thank them, too.
They smile; they cheer; they stand
and applaud; but are they really
seeing you?

Very soon you will not hear them.
Only a few will call your name.
In their eyes the star will have faded,
but to me you'll be the same.

It is a time of magic and wonder
accompanied by great celebration.
Then sad, slow moments - never ending
sorrow follows jubilation.

Empty feelings - something's lost.
All of the people have gone.
A bare stage - lonely players,
and yet the memories live on.

Conditional friends are behind you,
but please remember this:
your true friends are still beside you.
What you never had - you cannot miss.

Holiday Inn

Smelly cans of foamy beer,
diapers, and stale cigarettes.
These make us wonder why we're here
and why we stay with no regrets.

We get our share of grit and grime,
of muscle pulls, and backs that ache.
We sweep the dirt and wipe the slime,
and wonder how much we can take.

The work is hard and tips are slim -
we're lucky if they leave a dime.
Yet we're ever loyal to the Inn –
could we be out of our minds?

And yet if you look around
a little more then you will see
out of every place to work in town
this really is the place to be.

It has a special kind of feel
that you won't find just anywhere.
Our laughter is true
and our smiles are real.
We have a heart that really cares.

So what is the reason – is it pride?
Are we trying to beat out Super 8?
No, it's something even deeper inside
of each worker that makes us great.

The reason we give all we've got
and then strive to do even more,
the reason we love this place a lot
is because of the person we work for.

She's determined and she's strong.
She keeps everything flowing.
But it's not her orders - it's her smile
that often keeps us going.

Although she expects us to come through
with all our rooms done well,
she never forgets - we have feelings, too.
By what I write - you can tell:

When we are down and we frown,
and our strength is almost gone,
when we need some hope just to cope
and help us carry on -

Then we look to her to see us through
and our spirits start to rise.
She is always there and we know she cares
by the love that's in her eyes.

We'd like to thank you for your part
in making Phyllis our boss.
Without her humor and her heart,
we really would be lost.

Mary Kathryn: Dance the Dance

Dance, little girl, dance
while you still have the chance.
Now you are only two –
so much ahead of you.

But time travels fast –
so dance, little girl, dance.
Let me see you smile –
we're here such a short while.

It's your kindergarten play
and I can only pray
it'll always be this way
and you'll never go away.

The big high school dance –
dance, little girl, dance;
and enjoy every day.
Please remember me always.

It's now your wedding day
and I wish you could stay
my little girl forever –
we'd always be together.

But time travels fast –
so dance one last dance
with your dear old dad and
always remember the fun we've had.

Dance, little girl, dance,
we have this one last chance –
because my time is near
so please remember, dear,

Your daddy loves you so
and even though I have to go -
just as from the start
you'll always be in my heart.
Dance, little girl, dance.

Sweet Margaret

I hope you know how much I loved you?
I never actually told you so.
I'm lonely down here
and my heart is breaking.
Sweet Margaret, do you even know?

I know you are happy now and at peace
playing bingo and watching those Twins.
And up there it doesn't even matter
who loses or who wins.

Although I am happy for you, my friend,
I need a favor from you.
Could you please ask the Lord to send
an angel to see me through?

Because I could always count on you,
and I can't do this alone.
I am still down here on earth
while you're already home.

So, I need your prayers for a little angel
sent from above.
To give me strength, and acceptance,
comfort, hope, and love.

Although I can't see your smile
nor hear your voice,
I do feel your spirit here.
And the time we shared - our memories,
I will always hold dear.

You are a true friend and I am grateful
although you've passed through heavens door,
you will keep on loving me,
my sweet Margaret, forevermore.

The Visit

Here I am in the graveyard
where she was buried
one and a half years ago,
and I was too weak to come.

Wandering past the stones,
I search for her name.
What do I say if someone
asks me what I am doing?

"I'm looking for my friend, Margaret".
Then it hits me: a part of me is still
looking for her.
I'm hoping that I won't find her here.

Suddenly, I see her name.
The tears are falling fast -
so fast I can barely see
to place the cross I'd brought
for her into the ground.

Softly, I say, "Here you are.
You have a nice place to rest".
Then I hear her voice: "Cathy!
What're ya cryin' about? I'm fine.
Just get out there and live".

I smile and say, "Well, Margaret,
the first time is always the hardest.
The next visit will be easier".

I feel such pain knowing for certain
that she is gone.
Yet I also feel so much joy
knowing that her spirit and her love
continue to touch me and comfort me
even from the grave.

A Tribute

"Don't be a stranger",
I said to you
as I turned and walked away.
How was I to know that time
would be our very last day?

A part of me has mourned for you,
and longed to see your face.
Memories still linger
which time cannot erase.

Yet part of you is with me
in oh, so many ways.
I believe you always will be
until the end of my days.

Perhaps "don't be a stranger"
you really took to heart.
I feel your presence with me
as if we're really not apart.

You're with me at the bingo hall
where you'd complain you 'could never win'.
You're with me watching baseball games
and cheering on those Twins.

You're sending angels to me now
to give me rides and smiles.
To call me just to talk
and make life feel worthwhile.

Though I cannot see you with my eyes,
your love truly does shine through.
And I thank you, my sweet Margaret,
for the friend I still have in you.

Personal Sayings

I cannot think of anything more painful
than a broken heart
nor anything more blessed
than a heart that has loved
deeply enough to be broken.

Love

A moment without is an hour
While an hour with is but a moment.

Touch

Touch a stranger and share
Touch a friend and feel
Touch a lover and live.

Laughter leaps in the forest of friends;
respect rings true in the field of foes;
and love laps warmly on the ocean of
open hearts.

You know you really loved someone
when the pain is so overwhelming
that tears are not enough.

Life – a continuous series of beginnings
and endings.
Death – the ending and an eternity
of beginnings.

Love crowds your mind
warms your heart
and fills your soul with a feeling
of happiness, humbleness, and hope.

Sex

A union without love
is merely flesh upon flesh,
but a union out of love
is the ultimate ecstasy.

The heart that cries is not crying
to be filled, it remains full
by forever emptying itself of love.

If we could possess the innocence
of youth and the wisdom of the aged,
then each day could be a vision
and a memory.

Contentment

Thirst for water surmounted
by the thirst for victory.
Hunger for food filled
by the satisfied hunger
for love and appreciation.
Weariness of body banished
by the contentment of soul.
Seriousness and complications
of life surrendered
to the simplicity and serenity
of "togetherness".

Closing Words

Writing words for my writing class,
I stumble and I stutter.
"What do I write? What do I say?"
under my breath I mutter.

Somehow the words finally did come
and I believe I got an "A".
But more importantly I learned
the joy of writing on that day.

When feelings grew within my heart
until I thought I'd burst -
they'd overflow onto the paper
as rhythm, rhyme, and verse.

"My poems are for myself," I said,
when mom encouraged me to share.
I didn't think the world would listen;
read them; or even care.

Now with much love and support,
as surreal as it may seem -
I find myself publishing a book
and living out a dream.

Yet the poems are but 'reflections'
of God's goodness in this world;
and the people who have inspired them
are more precious than the words.

How humbling it is to know
that no matter what the art:
it is not now nor has it ever been
"How Great I Am"
but, oh, Lord - " How Great Thou Art!"